CODE ACADEMY

and the

Loopy Logic!

By Kirsty Holmes

BookLife

PUBLISHING

©2019
BookLife Publishing Ltd.
King's Lynn
Norfolk PE30 4LS

A catalogue record for this book is available from the British Library.

ISBN: 978-1-78637-553-7

Written by:
Kirsty Holmes

Edited by:
John Wood

Designed by:
Danielle Rippengill

IMAGE CREDITS

CONTENTS

Words that look like **this** can be found in the glossary on page 24.

REGISTRATION

Another day at Code Academy has begun.
Time for the register! Meet Class 101…

Bailey
Subject: **Memory**

Simon
Subject: **Coding**

Ashwin
Subject: **Programming**

Sophia
Subject: **Logic**

Frankie
Subject: **Debugging**

Jia
Subject: **Hacking**

Today's lesson is all about logic. We'll be finding out:

Ro-Bud
Subject: **Playtime!**

- What is logic?

- What are TRUE and FALSE?

- What is a decision?

- What is a process?

Code Academy is a school especially for kids who love computers... and robots too! Do I hear the bell...?

MORNING LESSON

This morning, the pupils at Code Academy have been building **supercomputers**. Bailey has been working on their project for ages.

```
If n=chocolate_cake
{return n+[frosting] , [sprinkles]}, engage:
slicing
          r={Bailey:hungry (break_time)}
{return n}, ice_cream
          <table><fork> href='/a'>a = 42
```

It's working! But now I'm hungry…

The class can't go to lunch until the classroom is spotless.

OK class, STOP! It's almost lunchtime, so it's time to stop working and tidy up.

LUNCHTIME!

This is going to take a while, and nobody wants to miss lunch. There are so many things to tidy up!

Cake!

Hardware!

Books!

Supplies!

Ro-Bud knows she has a set of instructions for tidying up. Jia **installed** them for her this morning. Instructions for a computer are called algorithms (say: al-go-rith-ums).

I can do it!

Frankie Fact:

Robots and computers don't need food or sleep, so they can keep working while people rest, eat or do other things.

The class comes back from lunch to find… an even bigger mess!

Ta-da!

11

TO THE WHITEBOARD!

Professor Chip takes the class to the whiteboard to think about the problem.

To find out why this program isn't working, we need to think about logic. Can anyone tell me what that means?

LOGIC

Sophia Says:

Computers follow programs to know what to do. Whenever the computer has to make a **decision** about something, it asks a question with a TRUE or FALSE answer. Depending on the answer, the computer will then know what to do next.

TRUE

FALSE

SOPHIA EXPLAINS IT ALL

Programs that use logic can be shown in a flow diagram.
Ro-Bud's computer has two choices:

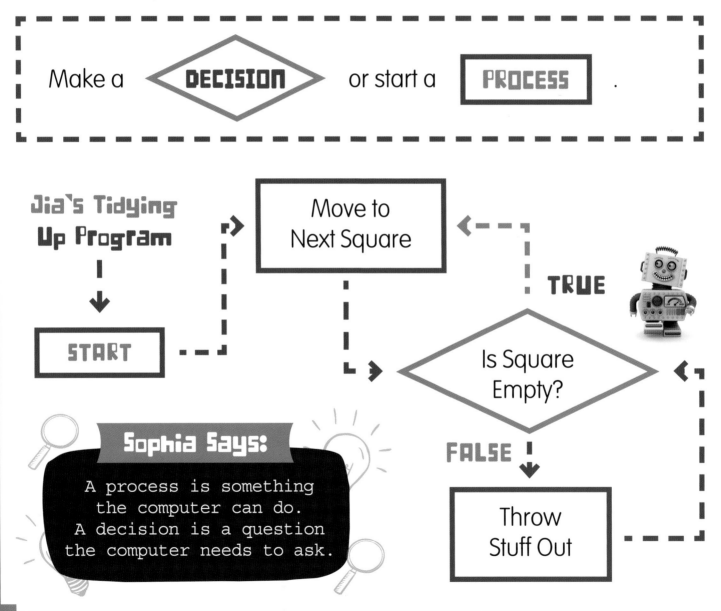

Make a **DECISION** or start a **PROCESS** .

Jia's Tidying Up Program

START

Move to Next Square

Is Square Empty?

TRUE

FALSE

Throw Stuff Out

Sophia Says:

A process is something the computer can do. A decision is a question the computer needs to ask.

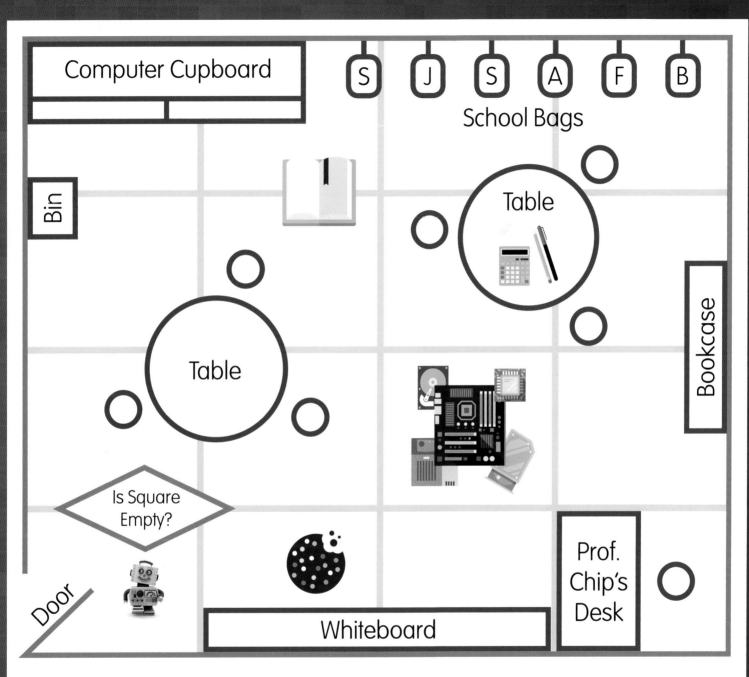

Ro-Bud sees the classroom as a **grid** of squares.
She needs to decide if the square she is in is empty or not.
Empty squares return TRUE and full squares return FALSE.

If the square is empty, the answer is TRUE and Ro-Bud will move on to the next square. If it's got something in it, the answer is FALSE.

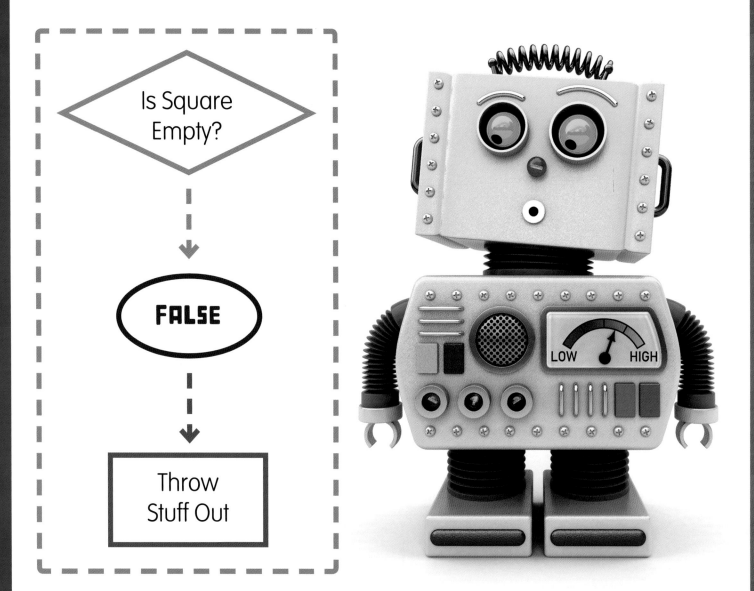

Ro-Bud follows the instructions Jia gave her exactly, so no matter what it is, Ro-Bud will put that item in the bin. Even Bailey's cake!

If we give Ro-Bud the wrong instructions, or if some are missing, she won't do what you expect her to.

SOLVE IT WITH LOGIC

So, how do we tell Ro-Bud what is rubbish, and what isn't?

Each time we add a logic question, Ro-Bud can get more information.

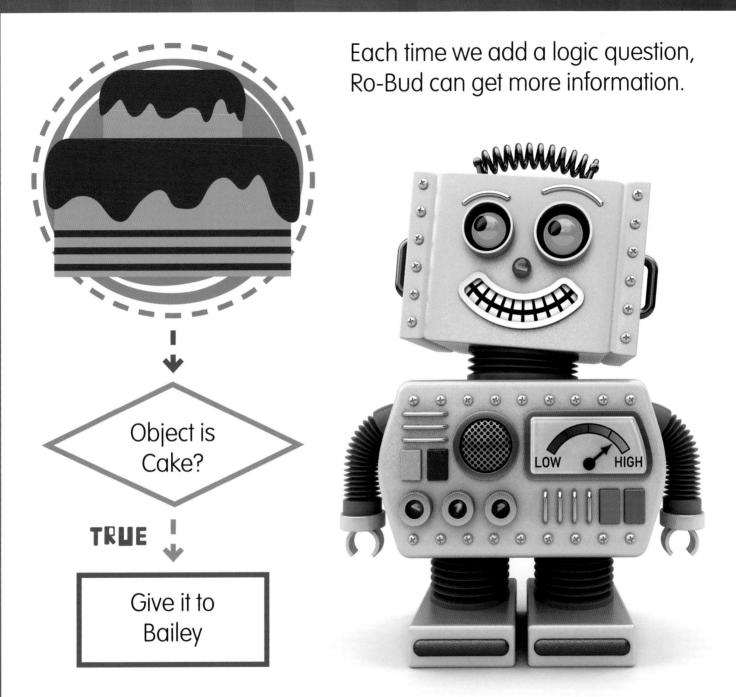

Object is Cake?

TRUE

Give it to Bailey

Each decision can have two processes: what Ro-Bud should do if the answer is TRUE and what she should do if the answer is FALSE.

Ro-Bud can ask all these questions very quickly.

All Jia needs to do is put the questions in the right order, and Ro-Bud will be able to decide what to throw away and what to leave alone.

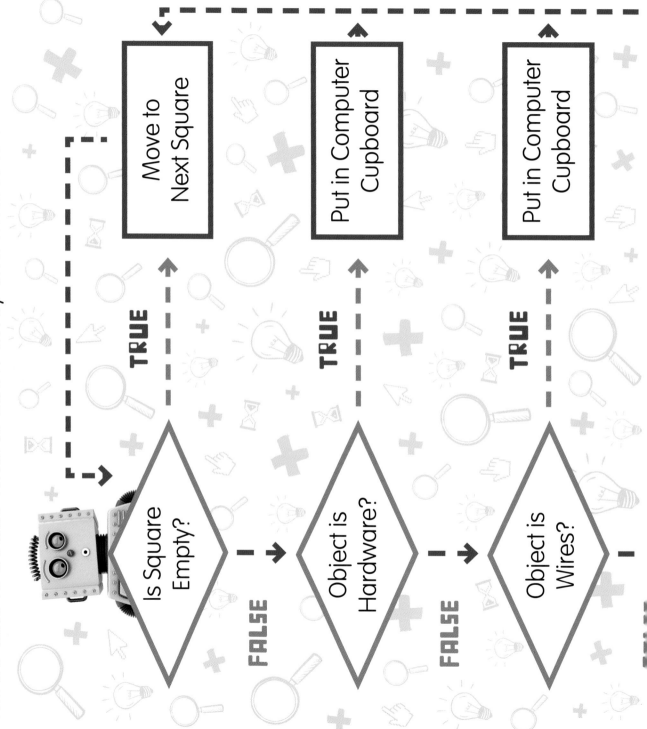

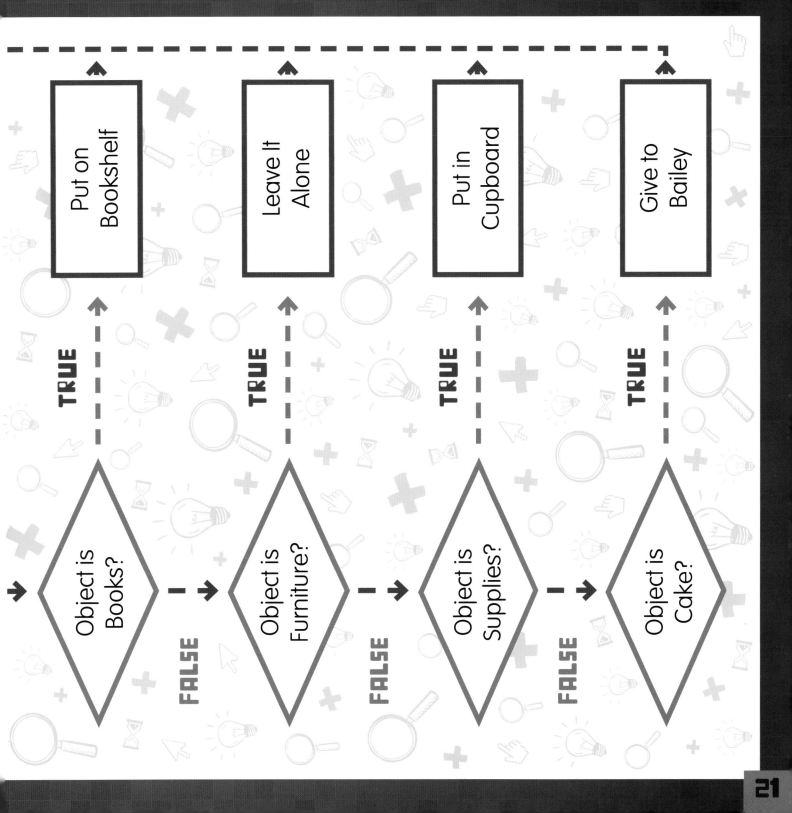

Object is Books? — TRUE → Put on Bookshelf

Object is Furniture? — TRUE → Leave It Alone

Object is Supplies? — TRUE → Put in Cupboard

Object is Cake? — TRUE → Give to Bailey

FALSE (between each)

ALL SORTED

Ro-Bud's new program works perfectly. Soon, with a little help from her friends, the classroom is absolutely spotless…

If only there was an algorithm to make this vacuum cleaner automatic…?

…for a little while, anyway!

HOMEWORK

Think of your morning **routine** when you get ready for school. Can you think of some logic questions to ask and processes to follow them? We've got you started, but can you add some more?

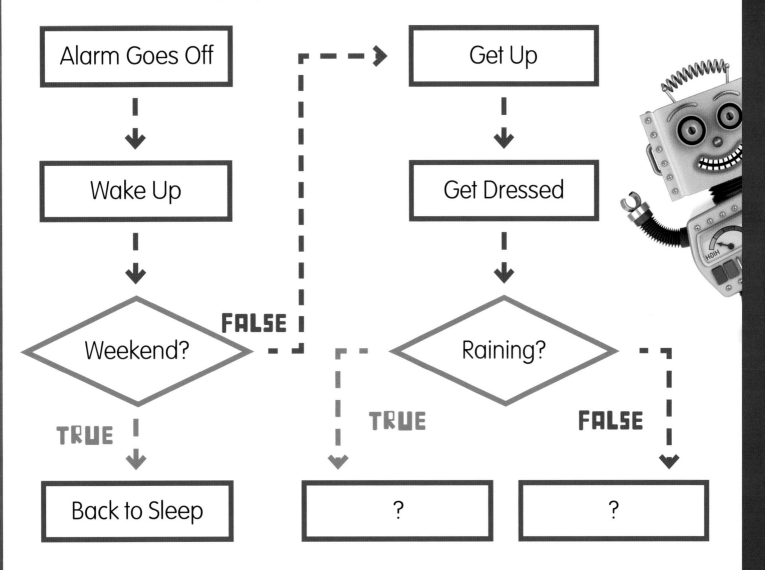

Alarm Goes Off → Wake Up → Weekend?
- FALSE → Get Up → Get Dressed → Raining?
- TRUE → Back to Sleep

Raining?
- TRUE → ?
- FALSE → ?

LOOK IT UP

GLOSSARY:

DECISION   when you have to choose one way or another

GRID   a pattern of lines which cross each other to make squares

HARDWARE   the parts of a computer that you can see and touch

INSTALLED   when something has been put into position, ready to use

ROUTINE   a set of steps that a person follows to get something done in the same way

SUPERCOMPUTERS   very powerful computers

INDEX: